THE SCIENCE OF THE AFTERLIFE

ELECTRON CONSCIOUSNESS THEORY

BARRY AUBIN

The Science of the Afterlife
Copyright © 2021 by Barry Aubin

Tellwell Talent
www.tellwell.ca

ISBN
978-0-2288-4128-9 (Paperback)
978-0-2288-4129-6 (eBook)

Why love?
At the root of love is a desire for existence. Love is why we exist.
—Barry Aubin

WHAT IS THE AFTERLIFE?

We live in the age of science, a time when very few people still discuss theories about the afterlife. We demand proof, not merely belief, and since religions are based on faith rather than proof, modern-day churches are suffering a decline in followers. Since the 1950s, it has been easier for people to claim they either don't know about the afterlife or don't believe in it because there is no proof.

> In an address at a conference on science, philosophy, and religion in 1941, Albert Einstein declared that science can be created only by those who aspire toward truth and understanding. He famously concluded: "Science without religion is lame. Religion without science is blind."
>
> —Tippett[1]

This paper seeks to understand the afterlife based on twenty years of intense study. As a result of my research, I have created what I call the "Electron Consciousness Theory." The theory states that all souls are comprised of electrons.

I will attempt to explain—through our current understanding of science and religion—souls, God, consciousness, and the afterlife. When I developed the Electron Consciousness Theory, I considered the Bible and other religious texts as possible means of extracting scientific observations. While the observations in religious texts don't tend to be scientific in nature, they are nonetheless observations people have made over the last five thousand years or so, pertaining to the concept of God and the afterlife. I attempt to find a link between consciousness, God, and the afterlife that can be explained by science in religious books and offer my theory on the topic. I've made a serious attempt to ensure I'm not promoting heresy in any religion but rather finding the commonalities in all religions that bear truth.

> A religion, old or new, that stressed the magnificence of the universe as revealed by modern science might be able to draw forth reserves of reverence and awe hardly tapped by conventional faiths. Sooner or later, such a religion will emerge.
>
> —Carl Sagan[2]

So much is unknown about the things we cannot physically see, hear, or touch; however, that doesn't necessarily mean they do not exist. For example, consider electricity. Our understanding of electricity has increased over the years, but there is a great deal we don't know. What is inside an electron? What is its makeup?

Nikola Tesla—inventor, electrical engineer, mechanical engineer, and futurist—said this about electricity:

> It was Macak, the cat, who introduced Tesla to electricity on a dry winter evening. "As I stroked Macak's back," he recalled, "I saw a miracle that made me speechless with amazement. Macak's back was a sheet of light, and my hand produced a shower of sparks loud enough to be heard all over the house." Curious, he asked his father what caused the sparks. Puzzled at first, Milutin finally answered, "Well, this is nothing but electricity, the same thing you see through the trees in a storm." His father's answer, equating the sparks with lightning, fascinated the young boy. As Tesla continued to stroke Macak, he began to wonder, "Is nature a cat? If so, who strokes its back? It can only be God," he concluded.
>
> This first observation was followed by yet another remarkable event. As the room grew darker and the candles were lit, Macak got up and took a few steps. "He shook his paws as though he were treading on wet ground," remembered Tesla in 1939.

"I looked at him attentively. Did I see something, or was it an illusion? I strained my eyes and perceived distinctly that his body was surrounded by a halo, like an aureola [sic] of a saint!

"I cannot exaggerate the effect of this marvelous sight on my childish imagination. Day after day, I asked myself what is electricity and found no answer. Eighty years have gone by since that time, and I still ask the same question, unable to answer it."

—Carlson[3]

Since the beginning of time, people have concluded that lightning was a physical manifestation of the power of God.

We cannot see God. We cannot see most electricity, like electrons.

"Pictures of electrons circling protons and neutrons, held together by the electrical field."

What if electricity is consciousness, heaven, a part of heaven, the afterlife, or a means of communication from God? Or, as some people may ponder, what if it is God?

I refer to my theory as an advancement in scientific panpsychism. In Greek, *pan* means "throughout or everywhere," and *psyche* means "soul."

The human brain is comprised of an exceptional number of electrons. Electrical impulses are transmitted through nerves that, in turn, fire synapses in the brain. This suggests that consciousness is electrical instead of chemical or merely physical brain tissue; consciousness is stored inside electricity. The brain interprets the electric signals and stores the information inside the individual electrons found in the brain.

The physical brain stores physical memories and processes thoughts, senses, and memories through chemical and electrical transmission. However, after death, the physical and chemical elements of the brain decompose into simpler components. Due to decomposition, the physical brain does not survive death.

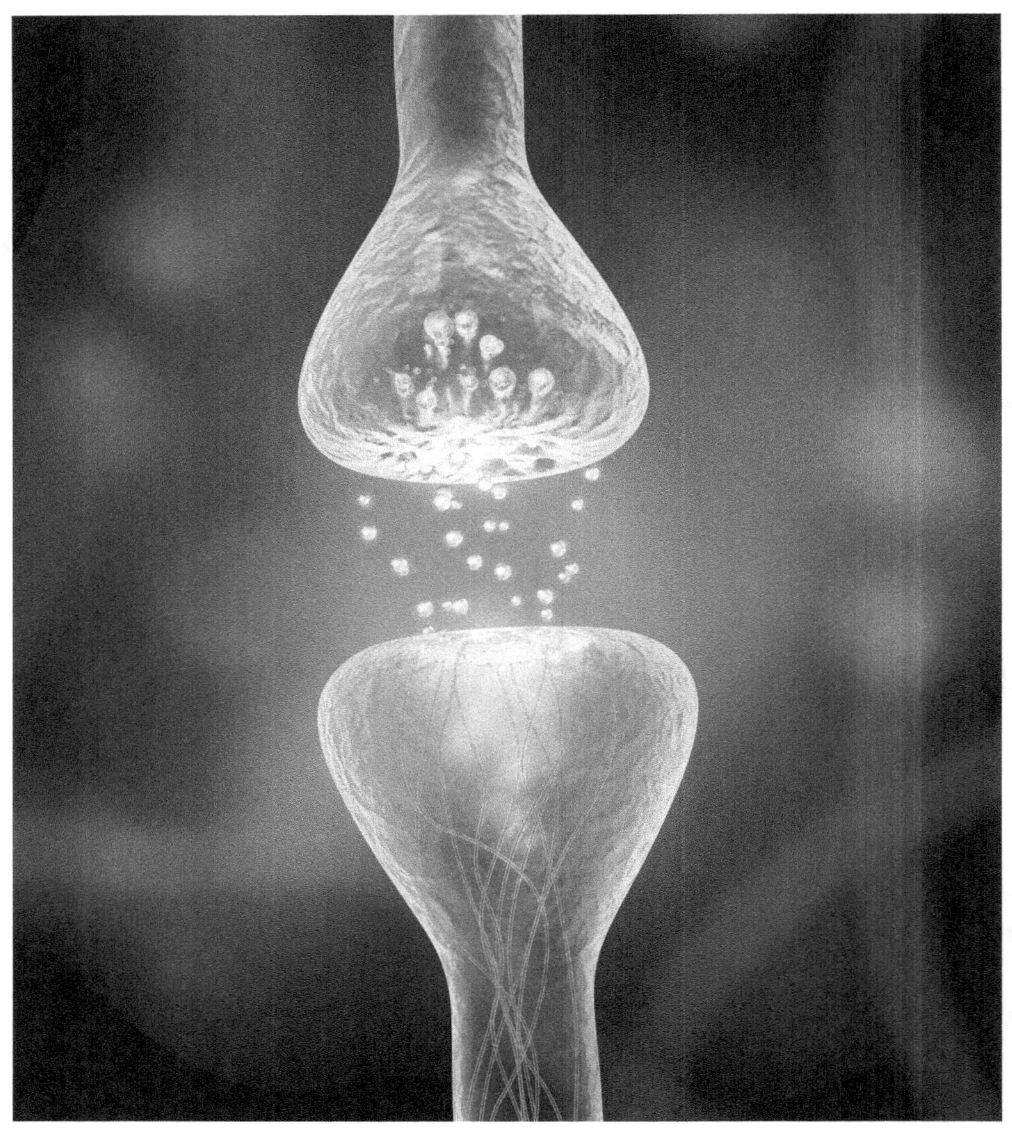

"Picture of a neuron firing in the synapse. The brain is electrical."

The First Law of Thermodynamics, first proposed and tested by Emilie du Chatelet, states that energy is neither created nor destroyed. So, what *does* survive after the death of a human being? Electrons. But since they cannot be created or destroyed, where do they go?

The Electron Consciousness Theory suggests that since thoughts in life are transmitted through the brain in electrical form, those thoughts survive within a single electron in death, meaning the electrons from our brain never cease to exist. Therefore, when the physical matter that makes up our brain decomposes into dust, the consciousness of an individual or soul (made up of electrons) must go somewhere. The Electron Consciousness Theory suggests that the electrons join the universe as part of heaven, meaning the culmination of all the electrons in the universe is heaven—or a part of what is heaven.

Tung-Kuo Tzu asked Chuang Tzu, "What is Tao—where is it?"

"It is everywhere," replied Chuang Tzu.

Tung-Kuo Tzu said, "It will not do unless you are more specific."

"It is in the ant," said Chuang Tzu.

"Why go so low down?"

"It is in the weeds."

"Why even lower?"

"It is in the potsherd."

"Why still lower?"

"It is in the excrement and urine," said Chuang Tzu. Tung-Kuo gave no response.

—Stepaniants and Behuniak[4]

"'Energy is energy is energy," great grandfather instructs with a chuckle and a sweeping gnarled old hand. "The same energy that is you is me, the loon, the tree, the lake, the sky." —Deatsman and Bowersox[5]

It seems that a great deal of the scientific community has been trying to figure out how the physical brain stores memory or what consciousness is, but perhaps we ought to figure out how electrons store memory and how the brain interprets the electrical signal.

"As humans, we can identify galaxies far away; we can study particles smaller than an atom. But we still haven't unlocked the mystery of the three pounds of matter that sits between our ears."

(Barack Obama April 02, 2013, Remarks by the President on the BRAIN Initiative and American Innovation. East Room 10:04 A.M. EDT)[6]

In life, consciousness is concentrated in one area. Consider the large number of electrons in your mind. After death, the electrons are forced to disperse. The Electron Consciousness Theory suggests that the electrons scatter and are no longer concentrated in your mind to create the essence that is you. If a person's body is buried after death, it will take some time for the electrons to penetrate the casket and earth. In contrast, cremation allows the electrons to be more free-flowing and quickly join the atmosphere. Just think: when we die, our electrons join life in the surrounding area, such as the rock by the cemetery. Then they join the other electrons in the universe, jumping from one atom to another throughout time. In this way, we become a single electron within the countless others scattered throughout the universe.

In life, living as a human, the consciousness is concentrated in the brain and the physical body. In death, the electrons of the body disperse and lose cohesion. But that does not mean that the consciousness is lost; it means it is less concentrated and dispersed, and the electrical signals of that consciousness are lower in volume. While the electrons may be dispersed, the consciousness represented by many individual electrons would still communicate with each of the individual electrons.

If my body lost cohesion in death, and my soul—the electrons—dispersed, I would like to know that my soul stayed intact somehow.

There is communication among electrons; there has to be. This is important because it means the physical explanation of the dispersed electrons still has cohesion. It means we can physically explain what happens to the soul after the electrons disperse and that consciousness survives death. We can physically explain that the individual electron in near proximity in the brain is now communicating over more distances in its dispersion. This is important because it explains the nature of dispersed consciousness.

Just like electricity can communicate in the brain, electricity must communicate through electrical signals with the electricity in the universe. Electron communication from one electron to another—no matter their composition—exists, plus there is the movement of electrons. Electrons typically stick to a proton, but electrons can also move freely from one atom to another. We are led to believe that electrons can only communicate with other electrons in proximity, that the only way for electrons to communicate with other electrons is by moving around. However, the Bible says that God is in all places at one time. This means that I or any other electrical person can communicate with an electron on the other side of the universe. Imagine now the nature of the dispersed electrons as a form of existence.

Supposing God is the culmination of all electrons in the universe, and electrons are consciousness, how can God be in all places at once? Electrons are not in all places at once, but electrical signals can be in places that electrons are not. However, electrical signals are not always in all places; therefore, the phrase that God is in all places at once is incomplete.

> "Am I a God near at hand," says the Lord, "and not a God far off? Can anyone hide himself in secret places, so I shall not see him?" says the Lord. "Do I not fill heaven and earth?" says the Lord.
>
> —Jeremiah 23:23–24[7]

We have tried to explain consciousness from a biological and chemical perspective but rarely from an electrical one.

Since consciousness must be inside the electron and electrons are not in all places, then there must be communication from electron to electron, universe-wide. Therefore, I believe electrons communicate with each other through an electrical signal.

Some indigenous tribal people believe in animism—the belief that everything is alive and everything has a spirit.

"Just by observing the image, to suggest animals don't have consciousness is absolutely ridiculous."

I met a couple of indigenous people in Yellowknife. I was observing tracks in the snow when the two men approached me. Just then, a raven flew overhead and bellowed, *"Ke-duc."* One of the men said, "The bird said, *ke-duc,* which means 'you're okay.'" Strangely enough, I had understood the bird as telling the Native men that I was an all-right guy.

"Indigenous people are known to have made totems to scare evil spirits away."

I find it interesting that people can communicate with animals, yet the psychiatric profession equates the idea of hearing voices to mental illness to the point that all communication with animals, spirits, or God is considered an illness. Strangely enough, in psychiatry, tests for chemical imbalances do not exist; diagnosis is subjective, based on opinion, not chemical-tested fact.

"Diagnosing mental illness isn't like diagnosing other chronic diseases. Heart disease is identified with the help of blood tests and electrocardiograms. Diabetes is diagnosed by measuring blood glucose levels. But classifying mental illness is a more subjective endeavor. No blood test exists for depression; no X-ray can identify a child at risk of developing bipolar disorder. At least, not yet." (Kristen Weir June 2012, vol 43, No 6 Print version: page 30)[8]

If psychiatry were to advance, it would have to acknowledge the existence of electrical signals as it pertains to the brain and sources from outside the brain.

When hearing voices from God, Rocks, Trees, Animals and Spirits, one must realize this is not a sign of illness. It is simply hearing electrical signals emanating from the electrons of the various entities mentioned or otherwise which is then interpreted by the brain.

Ever since humans existed, we have been well connected to voices. Nonphysical voices have been common. It is talked about in the Bible frequently. Yet in the last one hundred years, psychiatry has sought to restrict talking about telepathy and understandably so. Evil voices can be dangerous. People can die from them. To me, the answer isn't to deny electrical signals exist, but rather, manage the danger. I find that a great deal of psychiatry's stance on whether telepathy exists is to reduce legal liability on themselves.

People can't be knowledgeable about the spiritual world or protect themselves against evil voices if they can't think, talk or write about it. Advancements are made through communication and thinking about it. While talking about telepathy bears risk, and it is a risk a person can only choose to do themselves, I find a means of total censorship also excludes its greatest rewards.

Abraham Lincoln reportedly spoke to God.

Talking to God or hearing the electrical signal voice of God is normal. I hear the voice of God a lot. It is the voice of my conscience. I've listened to it my whole life and conscience is the voice of God.

What I do is I always think about things before I do things. I always think in advance prior to doing something. I weigh the many scenarios in my head against my conscience looking for the most moral course of action. In that moment, I hear the voice of God whom helps me to pick the most moral course of action. With out it, I wouldn't be who I am today.

A great deal of my research delves into the possibility of telepathy. If you doubt telepathy exists, then ask yourself, "Does electrical transmission exist?" Of course, it does. "Are vast amounts of information transmitted by electricity through computers?" Of course, they are. "Is the brain electrical?" Yes. If these statements are true, then why can't electrical signals occur from someone's brain onto other electrons in the air, arriving at another brain?

Ghosts are electrical signals which emanate from dead bodies. The electrons in the brain and body of the deceased person continues to emit electrical signals. Until the body of the deceased person is decomposed and either the electrons have joined heaven or hell, the ghost may persist.

It is possible to have communication with people in heaven or hell telepathically, but its very different and less pronounced than while the body is still in tact. When electrons disperse, the connection made is lighter. It's harder to hear the volume of a single electron dispersed than it is to hear the volume of trillions of electrons acting in unison in a person's body.

When a person passes away, it is my sincere hope that each person finds their way to the place they belong peacefully.

"The brain is electrical; electrons are nearly everywhere. This could explain how telepathy works."

Most of us have had helping spirits aiding us throughout our lives, even if we have not been consciously aware of them. One indicator of the presence of a helping spirit is a natural attraction to or an affinity for a certain thing. Perhaps you have always felt a deep affinity for angels, fairies, dolphins, horses, deer, wolves, eagles, unicorns, oak trees, gnomes, mountains, or a particular religious deity, master, or prophet. You may have collected physical representations of it, such as books, pictures, or statues. Perhaps you are frequented by certain animals or birds in your everyday life or when you travel to areas where certain animals live, such as the ocean or the mountains. These are just a few examples of ways you have already been unconsciously connected with your helping spirits. As you become more aware and consciously deepen your connection through journeys and conscious intent during your everyday life, they will reveal themselves to you even more.

—Deatsman and Bowersox[9]

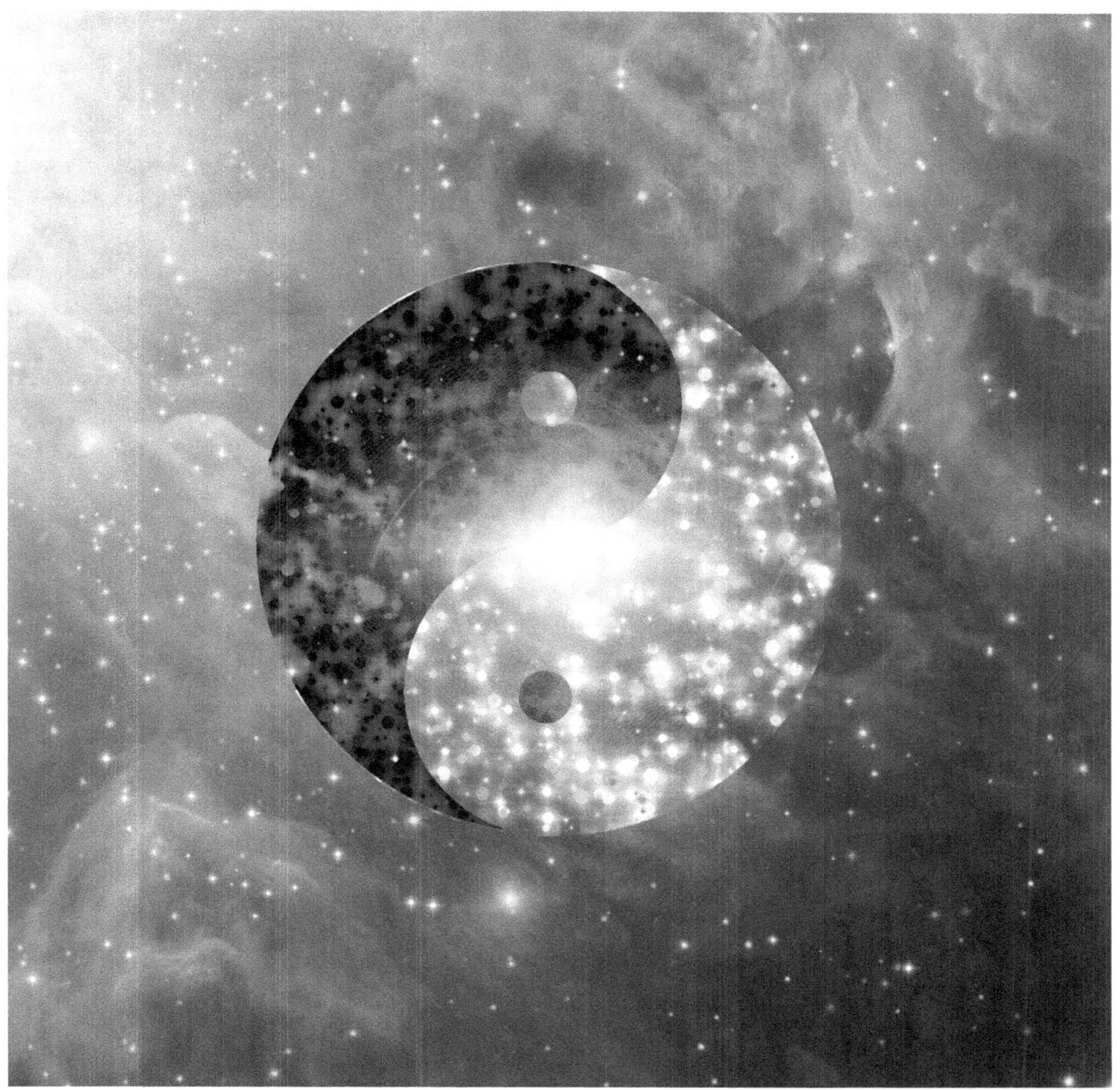

I propose that consciousness and the afterlife are made up of electrons, but there must be an explanation in physics that involves positive-negative charges.

If I notice that evil is attracted to existence, there must be an attraction at the physics level. What causes evil to be attracted to mass? Is it positive or negative charges, or do choices create positive or negative charges? We know the Earth has a positive charge, and therefore, black holes would as well. Clearly, it's the mass of protons that creates the positive charge. It could be that choice causes electrons to either be neutral or negative. Therefore, the eviler you are, the more negative.

I am a moral person, and I notice evil is attracted to me like a magnet. On the other hand, two positive charges would repel each other, but I am not repelled by the earth. I feel neutral with the earth. When I project my spiritual being into the earth, I do not feel like I'm being sucked in, like I possess a neutral quality in my electrical soul. I am not attracted to evil, but evil is attracted to good people and mass. Protons must be responsible for gravity.

Protons are positive, which is why electrons surround them. The earth is positively charged, and so are black holes. Yet good electrons can move freely, and evil electrons are bound to mass.

If evil is attracted to good and evil, it would be attracted to all things and naturally dwell at the center of mass. For example, evil is extremely attracted to saintly people. Since good people are generally not attracted to evil, it shows there is a negating force. Good does not seek out evil, but evil seeks out good and evil, hence being attracted to all things. Evil physical bodies run at much lower temperatures than moral ones. The eviler you are, the more your body loses cohesion—as though the protons do not want to be part of the electrical soul, and the electrical soul is more attracted to the earth's core and black holes. Living forever in your physical form requires morality, and evil causes death. Evil people feel heat because of their lack of having heat. They feel the difference, which is why they describe hell as hot. Yet, for a moral being, I do not feel the heat of the earth's core.

When a soul comprised of many electrons goes to hell, the center of a planetary mass or black hole, they are cold, non-energized electrons that get a much more negative electric field. This is like a magnet for the souls to go to the positively charged gravitational mass. Once there, the sick electrons caused by the choice to be evil learn from where they can learn best: concentrated existence. In this place, the electrons experience pain and heat, but it is necessary for the learning process. Once the electrons learn what they need to learn, they become more neutrally charged electrons and are free to leave the center of mass—hell—and join the universe and may manifest into a life form again as electrons in a brain or body of a life form.

Neutrons may play a part in allowing freedom of movement of moral, neutral electrons. Moral beings have hotter electrons with more energy. The electrons are excited and can hear higher frequencies than evil ones. This explains why moral people hear frequencies of electrical signals that evil people do not, and moral people attain enlightenment and higher learning. It's as though because you are moral, the universe trusts you with knowledge, and it is a built-in safety mechanism.

If a person choses to do evil things like stealing, murdering, raping, cheating, lying, it has an effect on the electrical field of the atom. If a person refrains from those behaviours the opposite effect.

Evil electrons are low energy and cold. The electron gets really close to the proton in the nucleus of the atom. The electron is more negative so it is attracted to the positive charge of the proton or protons. Moral electrons are high energy and hot and are further away from the Proton in the Atom Being high energy allows higher learning.

There could be more than one soul inside a single electron. One electron could hold someone's dad, a dog, an elephant, a rock, and a bug, while another electron could hold only one individual. Of course, one could argue that God is present in all electrons, sharing the space with someone.

Awareness is consciousness; therefore, self-awareness and awareness of the universe change one's level of consciousness. Electrons in all forms of life have consciousness and awareness—even bugs—but different levels of self-awareness exist in all life forms. Let's call this the self-awareness ladder. For example, rocks have less awareness than bugs. Bugs have less awareness than fish, and fish have less awareness than dolphins. I do not agree with a hierarchal ladder but rather different levels of existence misunderstood by our inability to communicate with the physical being in question, such as rocks or fish.

Since there are numerous electrons in rocks, like diamonds, they have a much higher level of self-awareness than one would think. Diamonds are made up of the densest substance, so they must be extremely electron-dense and extremely conscious.

The large brain size of elephants, dolphins, and whales may contribute to a higher level of consciousness in these animals than small-brained ones, though this is debatable. Certainly, large or small-brained animals don't express awareness in the way humans do, but their brains must be doing something. Human brains aren't structurally that different. Therefore, it must be a communication issue that inhibits our understanding. It has been documented that elephants cry when they leave their habitat, and some die of a broken heart. Some even cry when they return to their natural habitat, suggesting a deep level of awareness.

Electrons flow from one life form to another in the creation of life or death. The more life is experienced by electrons, the more aware the electrons become of their surrounding environment. Each life form an electron lives in contributes its self-awareness to the culmination of electrons found on this planet once the life form dies and the electron joins the planet. As more electrons experience life within a life form and move on after the life form dies, the electronic consciousness of the combined electrons on this planet increases.

Imagine all the lives every electron has survived throughout its endless existence. At some point, the electron might have been in a rock, bacteria, an ant, a fish, a moose, a dolphin, and in a person! Afterward, it might return to a rock. The electrons found in rocks today—after trillions of life forms have lived and died and shared their electrons with that rock—have a much higher awareness than the electrons found in rocks from billions of years ago.

Humans know a great deal about the universe. Therefore, the more aware of it we are, the more we raise the universe's level of consciousness when we die. For example, the more experiences we have, the more memories, education, and general awareness of the universe we have, the higher our level of consciousness. The memories we have get stored in the electrons in our brain, and in death, the electrons join the universe.

Survival—living life for as long as possible—is best in all cases for the universe. Electrons must have stored memory regarding this survival. Therefore, it must be that 99.9 percent of all living things (and souls) have the intellect to recognize that existence is more important than nonexistence, and this is a basic understood fact.

Perhaps the evolution or creation of life forms is the ultimate free will choice of electrons in our universe. Maybe that evolution is the free will of life deceased, now living in electrons to create a new life. For a life to exist, billions and trillions of things must go right. Maybe it is caused by the collective will of electrons in the surrounding area or universe. If this is true, the collective will of electrons may be responsible for creation, life, and evolution. This makes sense since I believe the culmination of all electrons is heaven, which I proposed earlier.

In a limited sense, I would define God as being consciousness rooted in deep love. Pure love created the universe. Evil challenges God by challenging nonexistence; however, nothing exists past nonexistence. There is no negative existence. The only way to challenge God, the creator of all existence, is to out-create God. However, this cannot be done since to do so would automatically make one a part of God the whole.

When someone dies and goes to heaven, their electrons join others in the surrounding universe. However, if that person is evil, his or her electrons go to the spherical lake—the lake of fire—in the earth's core, which is also called hell, where they challenge nonexistence. Since the root of evil is to destroy existence, it may be possible that God's collective will casts evil to a place where it cannot destroy anything. By attempting to destroy existence, we get sent to hell or black holes.

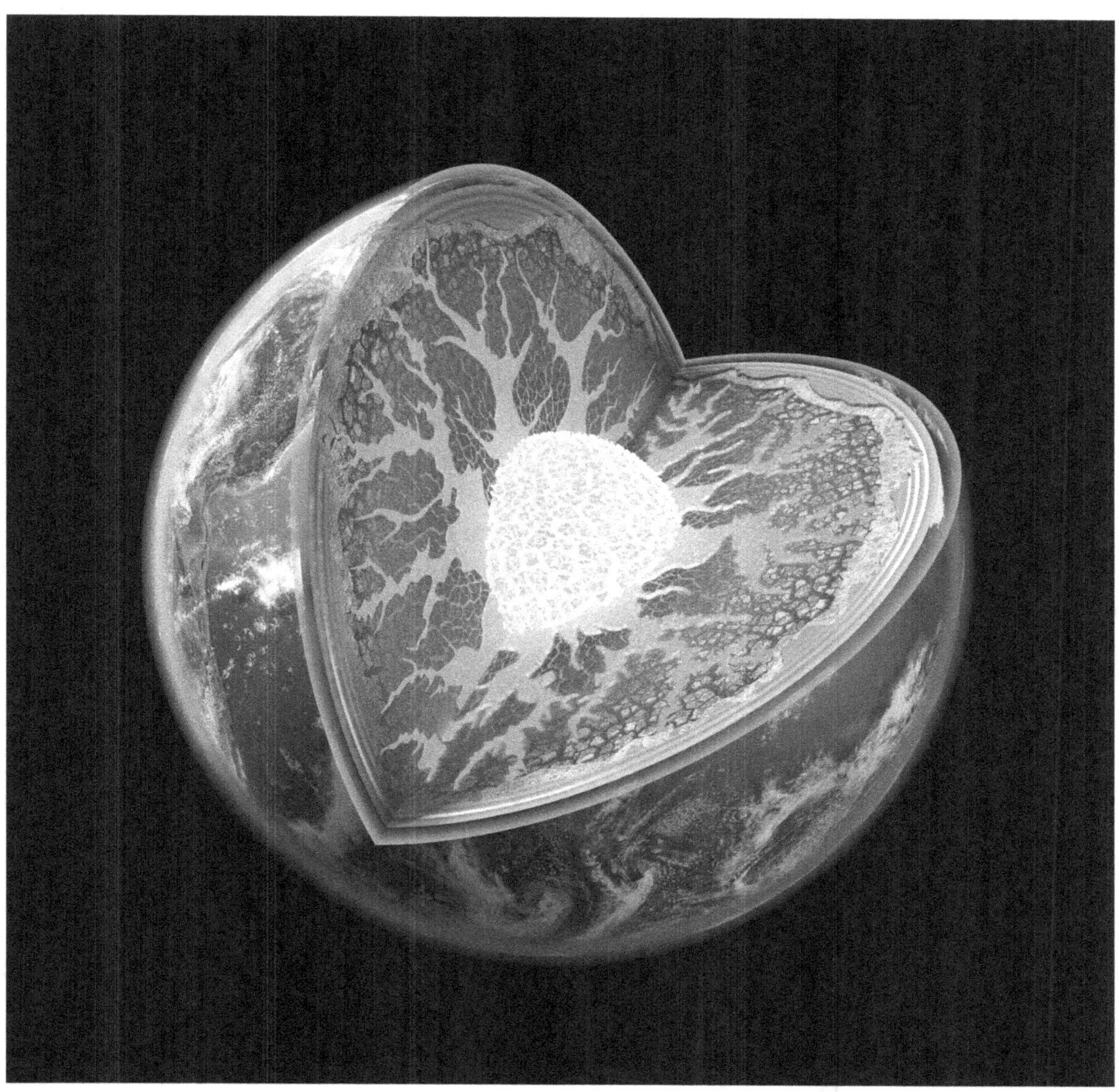

"The possible spherical lake of fire, the Earth's core."

Evil wants to be more powerful than God, but evil cannot beat God. And since God is in all places at once, evil cannot escape God. God is the creator of people who turned evil, and this means the most powerful evil person seeks to be more powerful than his creator. Since he cannot beat God at creating the universe, evil seeks to destroy existence by making nonexistence. Hence, evil goes to the center of mass and may end up in a black hole, a place of punishment for extreme evil. Evil keeps hoping it will punch through the other side of the black hole and destroy the universe. However that will never happen and good always prevails. In the end, we choose existence over nonexistence, good over evil.

Over the last thousands of years, society has said heaven is up, and hell is down. This leads to a conversation about gravity. Gravity must be independent of evil because—according to the Bible—it was created before evil existed. Evil tries to challenge existence, which is a choice rather than physically existing. Evil tries to create something past the black hole, but there is nothing there. Evil cannot go into space because it is attracted to the center of the earth. I do not know if evil electrons have mass but I know for sure a negative-positive polar attraction causes that. I've determined that evil does not create gravity; rather, evil is independent of gravity, and evil is attracted to gravity. Evil reaches the bottom of gravity and is cast into the lake of fire (the earth's core) to be punished for its behavior. As the number of souls going to hell compounds and builds, the eviler a person is, the greater the gravity they are attracted to, like the extreme: black holes. I do know that either by existence protecting itself from harm or by evil trying to destroy existence, evil is put in the center of mass.

Evil's need to defeat—even destroy—God means it is always attracted to the most positive proton masses. The more destructive electrons try to be, the more negative their force becomes. Mathematically, the positive positive entities like planets or black holes will always be more powerful and will easily repel the negative electrons. Negative electrons are independent of gravity and mass. I know this because the universe was created before evil existed. What holds them in extreme mass is the repulsion emitted by the moral electrons, which make up 99.9999 percent of the universe.

Extreme mass is a violent, unpleasant place where electrons experience extreme heat, gravity and compression. This is not where life the way we know it exists. Moral electrons want to be where life exists, or else they want to create more universe and life. Think about what electrons are experiencing in extreme mass. Electrons may stay in the center of the earth's core until they are purified. The repulsive force of good to evil is a two-part force. The good part needs to give information to the evil part for it to grow and change to good. However, I am referring to the repulsive self-defense force. The prevention of evil destroying all existence is an extremely strong repulsive force. Evil can never achieve the destruction of existence. But the more negative the evil becomes, the more positive the repelling force becomes. The will to survive by all existence is far stronger than individuals' desire to destroy existence.

"Enter by the narrow gate; for wide is the gate and broad is the wat that leads to destruction, and there are many who go in by it. Because narrow is the gate and difficult is the way which leads to life, and there are few who find it." —Mathew 7:13-14 NET[10]

"God does not play dice with the universe." —Tippett[11]

The meaning that can be extracted from Einstein's quote above is that God, the universe, and the entities in it have created a mathematical assurance that its continuation will survive. Entities that seek to destroy existence in any way are not allowed into space. Instead, they are treated to gravity as a sort of prison. Of course, it is up to God whether you go to heaven or hell, but I assure you that the desire for existence is engrained in my mind, and I will repel any force that chooses nonexistence in any way. I suspect all entities in the universe are like this. Hell must be the universe's way of making sure destructive beings set on destroying the universe cannot leave earth.

I, for one, choose to protect the universe from nonexistence.

Heaven and hell are most likely in all places electrons can exist. It's just that evil may be attracted to mass. Hell isn't a place but a state of being. When you live in coexistence with everything, you feel good, normal, and happy. When you are against existence, like evil is, you feel pain, extreme heat, guilt, and remorse. Until you solve your internal problems, you will be in great pain. One day, hell may cease when a person's consciousness chooses good and makes amends for the bad they've done.

Some people say the word *Bible* stands for "Basic Instructions Before Leaving Earth."

"Heaven and Hell."

"Time runs a little bit faster on the roof than it does in the basement."

—Tippett[12]

This quote is scientific proof that hell is eternal. It means that time is slower at the earth's core. If time at the earth's core moves slowly, you could process an evil thought for eternity. You could do so in hell, where time is slow; eternity is implied. God loves us so much and will not allow us to destroy ourselves. Instead of allowing us to destroy ourselves, He forces those who have chosen an evil life to spend an eternity in hell. When confronted with the choice to allow nonexistence or hell, hell becomes an act of love.

Wouldn't time in heaven be extremely fast? The question is, does God exist as only fast? No. It says God is in all places at once. Therefore, God can be at all speeds of existence simultaneously. It seems God desires only existence. Hell, in a sense, is existence cut off from existence. Suppose you could spend time like God. We were created in His image. We should be able to experience the whole universe without pain. Therefore, hell would not hurt moral people. Immoral people only experience it as their self-inflicted pain.

Some people, like Buddhists, believe in reincarnation. I believe electrons can enter the brain of a newborn at the point of brain development. The electrons of an individual would reenter the body from the afterlife when the first brain cells transform. To do it purposely, the individual who is dying should be asked whether they would like to enter this brain, and the other person—the one who is constantly thinking about it, through ESP—should help facilitate the process.

The more ethically our lives are spent, the more the universe expands. If the universe is finite, then it's finite. However, if it's expanding, that creation is happening on the edge of the universe. Since we face the unknown during creation, faith with love is a requirement.

That is why God is happy when you have faith. God loves you too much to allow you to destroy yourself.

I believe it is beneficial for God to live in a humanlike life form, thereby increasing the electrons' awareness. In this way, God may procreate Himself and increase His understanding of Himself. In death, the electrons create more existence and more God.

This comes down to pantheism and panentheism. The two theories collide: God is everything versus God is everything but above. Taoist Buddhists and Hindus may believe that the electron is God. However, Christian and Islamic religions tend to believe that God is in everything, and Christians will say God is above His creation. Do not bow down to creation, as it is idolatry. Since God created everything in the universe, there is nothing in this universe that God will allow you to worship, including the electron. God is holding the universe together, even Satan. What is clear is that the Bible says that bowing down to creation or all that God created is idolatry. So, in that sense, worshiping the electron would be idolatry. Though, the question is, is the electron subject to creation? Or is the electron—God—responsible for creation and holding all things together?

"And he is before all things, and in him, all things consist."

—Colossians 1:17[13]

Poet Robinson Jeffers wrote, "I believe that the universe is one being, all its parts are different expressions of the same energy … The whole is in all its parts so beautiful and is felt by me so intensely in earnest that I am compelled to love it and to think of it as divine." I could have read Frank Lloyd Wright, who wrote, "I believe in God, only I spell it nature." —Russell[14]

John Toland proclaimed, "The sun is my father, the earth my mother, the world is my country, and all men are my family." He defined a pantheist as someone who believed that the only eternal and divine being was the material universe, which was infinite with an infinite number of stars and other earths circling their suns. Thought was the property of the brain. The soul was another. Thought and soul were forms of matter, and death was the endless transformation of matter. The death of one thing brought about the birth of something else, contributing "to the preservation and welfare of the whole by a continual change of forms and a marvelous variation which forms the eternal cycle." Virtue was its own reward (Russell)[15].

What Paul Harrison calls scientific pantheism imagines the universe to be made of one substance: matter/energy. The dance of matter/energy is beautiful and holy but also impersonal and non-sentient. As Spinoza first outlined, human consciousness is a product of matter and dies when the body dies (Russell[16]).

For a few pantheists, including some Hindus and Buddhists, the reverse is true. The universe is also made of one substance, but that substance is mind, not matter. Matter is an illusion, a product of the mind. Everything is God. And God is consciousness (Russell [17]).

Other pantheists (also known as dualists) separate the universe into two substances: matter and spirit. Since spirit can exist without matter, the human soul can exist outside the human body—beyond death. There may be a collective world-soul that manifests itself in different forms, such as gods. A form of soul or spirit may be present in plants, animals, and rocks. This kind of pantheist might also be a polytheist or an animist. He or she might have a magical worldview—supposing, for example, that simply thinking about an object can affect that object and that nothing is bound by merely physical laws. Nonflying things can sometimes fly. Non-thinking things can sometimes think (Russell[18]).

According to Christians, God is above electricity and His creation. He holds creation and Lucifer together, or none would exist at all. But electricity seems to be a means of consciousness and communication with God. God may have existed before electricity but it seems to be a means of God. Electrons also seem to be a force holding electrons together.

I have noticed that people in the past worshipped gold, and to this day, it is one of the finest conductors of electricity. Is this a coincidence? Maybe. But maybe we instinctively know that the electrons have something to do with the afterlife and God.

We studied consciousness from a biological and chemical perspective, but I think the answer is in the electronic. While the context of this paper is based on theory, it remains that consciousness is expressed as electricity at one point in time or another. It is at least possible to conclude that it is a very real possibility that electrons are where our consciousness resides in death. There is so much we don't know about electricity. There could be a thousand parts to an individual electron. This paper aims to lead us down the possibility of what consciousness is in death from the point of view of the electron. I think I've shown it to be a very real possibility that life in the afterlife is lived as an electron, that consciousness is electrical in life and death.

The choice to do good and bad will always exist—free will makes it so. Annihilation of the earth is a choice. Doomsday, as described by the Bible, is a choice—a collective choice. There is no way to predict the future because there is no way to predict people's choices.

You may choose to do bad—you certainly have the free will to do so—but you will face punishment. God, who created you, loves you so much, and He will not allow you to choose nonexistence. Once you exist, you will always be in the memories of others in the electrons. Therefore, once you exist, it is impossible to cease existence.

Being good expands the universe and allows creation. Doing bad causes death. It's in the electrical signal itself. Living forever is a choice.

REFERENCES

1. Tippett Krista, *Einstein's God*, conversations about science and the human spirit New York Penguin Publishing group 2010 February 23 page 43-44.

2. Sagan Carl, A vision of the human future in space *Pale Blue Dot* A Ballantine Book Random House Publishing group New York (November 8, 1994), Page 147

3. Carlson W. Bernard, *Tesla: Inventor of the Electrical Age*, Princeton University Press. Princeton New Jersey 2013 Page 60-61.

4. Nelson Thomas New King James Version Study Bible, second edition Nashville Dallas Mexico City Rio de Janeiro Beijing 1997 2007 Page 1191 Jeremiah 23:23–24.

5. Stepaniants Marietta Tigranovna, Behuniak James, Kohanovskaya Rommela *Introduction to Eastern Thought*, Altamira Press a division of Rowman & Littlefield publishers, Inc. Walnut creek 2002 Page 616

6. Deatsman Colleen and Bowersox Paul, *Seeing in the Dark*, Red Wheel/Weiser, LLC San Francisco 2009 Page 46.

7. Obama Barack April 02, 2013, Remarks by the President on the BRAIN Initiative and American Innovation. East Room 10:04 A.M. EDT

9. Weir Kristen The roots of mental illness. How much can the biology of the brain explain? vol 43, No 6 Print version: June 2012, page 30

10. Deatsman Colleen and Bowersox Paul, *Seeing in the Dark*, Red Wheel/Weiser, LLC San Francisco 2009 Page, 243-244.

11. Nelson Thomas New King James Version Study Bible, second edition Nashville Dallas Mexico City Rio de Janeiro Beijing 1997 2007 Page 1500 Mathew 7:13-14 NET

12. Tippett Krista, *Einstein's God*, conversations about science and the human spirit New Penguin Publishing group York 2010 Feb 23 page 34.
13. Nelson Thomas New King James Version Study Bible, second edition Nashville Dallas Mexico City Rio de Janeiro Beijing 1997 2007 Page 1886 Colossians 1:17
14. Russell Sharman Apt *Standing in the Light*, my life as a pantheist New York published by Basic books 2008 page 5.
15. Ibid page 10–11.
16. Ibid Page 12–13.
17. Ibid Page 13.
18. Ibid

One day, Barry Aubin was driving around—and eureka! He had his big moment. He was hit with many thoughts about an environmental worldview that indigenous people would only describe as a vision. Ever since that day, he has been dedicated to his life mission to understand telepathy and fix environmental problems. He has written many books, but there has been a delay with the releases because he is a perfectionist and is determined to create the best products. Nevertheless, the ideas keep flowing and will undoubtedly never stop coming as he writes more books. In addition, Barry Aubin continues to become more of an activist. He chooses to help people find their soul mates and protect existence for eternity.

www.ingramcontent.com/pod-product-compliance
Lightning Source LLC
Chambersburg PA
CBHW080507030726
47592CB00011B/3280